Wobble

Bruce Conklin

DEDICATION

To my beautiful wife who believed in me and allowed me to pursue my passion and career, while taking the major role of mother to my six incredible children.

To my clients who put up with my constant pressure and resolve in invoking change, and even when they weren't sure it was the right direction still put in the dedicated effort to achieve results that collectively we couldn't have imagined.

To my colleagues who put up with my driving them to work the long intense hours to achieve great results and their courage to allow the process to teach them to appreciate the satisfaction in creating something new.

To my mentors along the way who prepared me to successfully take on the challenges in my mid-forties in the crisis and turn-around field, which turned out to be my true passion and purpose in life.

CONTENTS

Forward

FORWARD

Wobble:

Webster definition: unsteady movement from side to side

Conklin definition: when businesses begin to teeter after surges in growth and/or when undetected tremors and quakes create havoc.

The purpose of this book is to reach out to CEO's and owners of lower middle-market companies (under $100M annually) who might be in need of re-energizing their business and stemming the tremors.

After having the opportunity of working with CEO's for 25 years, I am always in awe of their fierce competitive drive and seemingly endless energy towards a goal.

One of my early clients, whose CEO remains a friend to this day, told me what he remembers most about working with me was my bringing a calmness and order to the crisis and ultimate turnaround. I enabled him to remain focused on selling the company and always knowing when he got back to the office everything would be okay. This is the highest compliment I have ever received.

This book is a quick read. Hopefully it will raise more questions and things to think about. If all else fails, perhaps I will get a chance to meet you.

CHAPTER 1

King of the Castle

Bob always liked to believe he was self-made, since he came from middle class working parents, who had worked at one company their entire life, and attended a state university on an athletic scholarship.

After going through marriage counseling for the first time, he decided to seek individual counseling, which provided a major breakthrough in understanding his behavior patterns. Bob was a perfectionist, procrastinator and fiercely independent, the last being most likely an over-reaction to domineering parents.

Like a lot of kids growing up in the 60's and 70's, he dutifully went to work at a large chemical company out of college and married his senior year sweetheart. Before most of his friends, he was able to buy a house and began living life as a commuting worker.

He was good with people, had a great work ethic and soon

moved up in the ranks, but increasingly was becoming frustrated since he had different ideas and was not comfortable with the slowness at which the company made progress and change. He was further frustrated by having to work with co-workers who didn't share his same values and intensity for success.

At 35, with two children and a newly increased mortgage from purchasing his first move-up house, he left the corporate world and embarked with a colleague on creating a distribution company to expand a niche market that his predecessor company had abandoned.

Bob learned through two recessions and near divorce that success was obtained through hard work and never giving up. He spent six days a week and 12-hour days building the business, but along the way also out grew his partner. Taking on additional debt, he bought out his partner at an inflated price, just to get rid of him, confident that he could make up the value through market growth.

That's when he took on the asset-based debt structure that he had, many times larger and more expensive today, that propelled him to more than double his size in the last 10 years.

Although he had been successful, he often wished he had more of a financial mind. He noticed in his YPO group (Young Presidents Organization) that many of the executives had a better feel for their balance sheets and were able to put together well thought out business plans. In his perspective, what they lacked, in many cases, was his "seat of the pants" vision and work ethic.

Over the years, Bob had assembled a pretty good business team. Glenn was a great salesman and closer. What he lacked in administrative and mentoring skills, he compensated by getting into the field and helping other salesmen close deals.

Bill, the general manager, excelled at the manufacturing and distribution, having been trained at another similar size company. Bob could always rely on him to get the product out the door.

Jane, the controller, had been with him since the beginning, originally starting as a clerk, rising to accounting manager, and then getting the promotion to Controller when the previous employee of only two years quit, after coming to odds with the team. He could always count on her loyalty and support in team meetings.

Life was good. Bob was pulling down a great salary and was now able to enjoy more free time with his great passion of car racing. Two children, from his previous wife, were now through college. His last child, a junior in private school, was doing well and looking to go to his same alma mater.

Everything was great …. Like a *spinning top!*

But he was not ready for what would come next.

Takeaways:

- Bob had made it as a businessman, but was beginning to spend more time with his outside interests and *getting away from what created success, dogged hard work and innovation. Can he create and delegate this to his team?*

- Bob's management style is autocratic, demanding loyalty. *Will he get the real truth from his intimidated management team?*

- Bob had leveraged his business — *asset-based lending arrangements help growing businesses by creating liquidity quickly. Likewise, when they level off or decrease, they consume liquidity just as quickly. Is there an adequate "navigational" tool to predict?*

- Bob is independent and self-sufficient. *Will he be able to utilize outside help on a strategic basis to help manage the growth?*

CHAPTER 2

Everything Was Fine Last Month .....

Glenn was a genius at sales. He had been in the business for over 20 years and really knew how to sell "solutions" to the customers. He was a former athlete and knew how to work with a team. All in all, he was a perfect VP of sales.

He had made a great living, even though he had been passed over for the CEO spot. Generally speaking, he had a great family. He had put his son through college and his daughter was a senior in high school. He could still fit into his high school letterman's jacket.

They had just finished a second consecutive year of sales increases, (although sales had been flat for the last 3 months, nothing to panic about) the product line was well laid out and backlog was the largest it had been in 3 years. Their next four months of sales goals were 80% covered. The salesmen's commissions were increasing and everyone was happy.

As the Company increased in size, so did their market-share. There were rumors that two new competitors had entered into their market space. Two of their customers had already begun sourcing from them.

It was early in the morning and he had just finished his favorite café latte and blueberry scone, when the phone rang. It was his favorite customer and long-time friend, with whom he had gone to college. Their wives knew each other and they had been on family vacations together.

"Hey Glenn, I have been meaning to call you for several months now, my production is getting messed up because we are running out of critical parts. My purchasing manager says it's because of a rise in partial shipments and missed dates, pushing our production schedule out of whack. I'm now getting pressure from the old-man and I assured him you would get on it."

He had no sooner hung than he got a call from John, his number one sales rep in New York. "Glenn, I was following up on that receivable problem with AcuTrue Industries that you spoke about at last week's sales meeting. It turns out that they are holding invoices on all partial orders. There is even talk that there may be back-charges for missed shipping dates which have halted production on their side. I need resolution with this or it could get ugly."

It was still early and maybe Bill, the general manager, was in his office. Glenn thought about calling him, but decided it might be better in person, so he re-filled his coffee cup with regular coffee from the lunchroom and headed out to the plant.

Bill was sitting in his office with the shipping and production managers going over the rest of the week's shipping and plant production schedules. He was about to track down the purchasing manager, when Glenn entered the office.

"Glenn, I know why you are here. I guess I'm surprised you haven't talked to me sooner, but I know what you're going to say. I have been getting calls for the last few weeks from your sales guys about late and partial shipments. I want you to know this is not my fault. We can't get material from our suppliers on a regular basis, some are on COD and others are hearing rumors in the industry. They all want their past-dues paid or they're going to stop shipping. I spoke to the controller and he says we have a temporary cash shortage issue."

Glenn slumped back to his office. "How could this be happening," he thought, "just when we were getting our act together and growing?" He was the most senior officer and carried the most weight below the owner and CEO, Robert.

It wasn't long before Glenn knew Bob needed to be looped in on the looming crisis.

Bob had often described a well-run organization as a *spinning top,* gathering momentum and working like a well-oiled machine. This was going to be his first real challenge, and one in which he had no experience.

This was the first *wobble* he had seen in his 10 years with the company. He was for the first time nervous about his career, after all he had just bought a new house and his wife was bent on putting the kids in private school.

Takeaways:

- Sales staff had all been making quotas and more compensation than they could have hoped for, during the last 3 years of growth. *Had they really become "order" takers? Would they be able to really make sales calls again?*

- Competitors were entering the market. *Did they really have a strategy to combat this? How do they differentiate themselves and become "the" solution to their customers?*

- Stock outs and late deliveries were becoming the norm. *There is already a perception in the market that they are in trouble. How do they overcome this perception with their customers? How is their competition using this?*

- Dilution was now a consideration. *How is this going to affect margins, his salesmen and his compensation?*

CHAPTER 3

The Scramble

Bob called a staff meeting over lunch. Glenn, Bill and Jane were all present.

"What do you mean we haven't paid the vendors?" he screamed? "Are we behind with KT Plastics?"

"Yes, and they want $90,000 in past dues paid before another shipment," chimed in Jane the Controller. "We are also past due with most of the others as well, but I have most of them under control."

"What do you mean under control?" queried Bob. "I have payment plans, post-dated checks and quasi-COD arrangements set up with the critical vendors. Only one non-critical vendor is threatening suit, and we have five vendors in collection," answered Jane.

"How did we get here without my knowing this?" asked Bob. "I thought we just had a budget meeting last month."

"We did and I told you we were maxed out on our

borrowing base with the bank. You said not to worry, that you would speak with our loan officer," replied the controller.

Jane went back to her office after the staff meeting and saw the message lights on her phone blinking. She already knew what they were - angry and confused vendors, who had begun calling her steadily for the last three weeks.

She had given her accounts payable clerks the "company line" to answer questions, but the vendors wanted to speak with her personally. She knew it was just a matter of time until they began calling Bob, especially the ones that had a personal relationship with him.

Reluctantly, she began listening to the, now, 30 messages that she had not listened to for the last three days.

One of the messages, left two days ago and sandwiched in between the vendor calls, was from Henry, the asset-based lender. He was wondering where the financial statements were, he had some questions about the borrowing base and the account was in a small over-advance position due to checks that they had allowed to clear.

Jane was beside herself. "What do I do?" she thought. "This is serious. What do I tell Robert? He is going to be upset."

She knew she was headed into a nuclear war, but she had to tell the CEO. There was no way she was going to make the call to the bank without him, especially when he had just played golf with the President of the bank a few weeks ago.

"Hey Bob, do you have a few minutes?" she said after knocking on his door. "Just a few, I have to meet with Glenn on some sales issues," he replied.

After downloading the bank voice mail, Bob decided to call Henry first thing in the morning. She was surprised at how well he took the potential disaster and happy he did not yell at her. He could be very emotional and did not like surprises. Especially bad news!

Takeaways:

- Past due vendors and COD – *as business decreases, vendors want old invoices paid first (which are lower than current run-rate). Where will this cash come from?*

- Post-dated checks and float – *how do they manage this with an already over worked staff? What happens if they bounce a check?*

- Maxed borrowing base – *no wiggle room left for "oopsies." What do they do, especially now that they are in their slow season?*

- Surprise to banker – *company credibility now challenged. What will the bank do now that they think the business is out of control?*

CHAPTER 4

The Call

Henry, their long time banker, was relieved to receive the call, so he didn't have to make the first inquiry. He hated this part in the lending relationship.

He was nervous and was especially concerned that the financials were late and that there was no availability in the line with the slow season looming.

Bob took this opportunity to tell him that the financials would be forthcoming but he was fearful that there would be a loss for the month of January and that there would be a few, year-end adjustments that he had not anticipated. Henry said he wasn't surprised, but that it was soon going to be off his plate, since the loan was going to be moved to special assets, but not to worry since they would work closely with the company.

After hanging up, Bob was now nervous. He had a few fellow YPO'ers whose companies had gone into special assets. One had to sell his company and the other had to get new financing. All they could do was wait.

Was the *spinning top* beginning to *wobble?*

They didn't have to wait long, because later that afternoon, they both received an email introducing them to Hugo, the special assets person. He requested they produce the January financials and a projection for the rest of the year, including covenant and borrowing requirements. He also wanted to see a current aging of accounts receivable, inventory and accounts payable. He was going to have an auditor visit the company to review receivables and update the inventory appraisal.

In addition, he had added a provision to hire outside help, and had attached the names of three potential firms who were on their approved advisors' list.

Needless to say, Bob's first reaction was one of anger. When they chose this lender it was mostly because of their assurance that they would be a *partner* and help them grow and get through the potential *land mines* that come with small businesses.

"Where are they now that I really need them? Should I call the president?" wondered Bob. After thinking this through for a moment, he agreed to get the bank what they needed, to begin interviewing the potential candidates and meet with Hugo and Henry in a few weeks.

Bob wondered if this was the *wobble* his fellow YPO'ers often spoke about? Could this truly be happening to his company?

Takeaways:

- Late financials – *usually an indication that allocations and unexplained variances are holding up the process. What hidden costs and losses had they not reconciled?*

- Special assets – *usually the sign of lender fatigue – will they be forced to find another lender? Are they going to freeze the line?*

- Inventory appraisal and receivables audit – *if the appraisal is lower, then the line may be over-advanced? Will they increase the reserves for dilution?*

- Crisis Manager – *how are they going to pay for this? What will the employees think when he steps in the building?*

CHAPTER 5

Welcome to Crisis

Bob was alone in his office. Everyone had gone home.

Bob angrily wondered why Glenn, Bill and Jane weren't burning the midnight oil and sharing his assessment of the looming crisis ahead.

"How can I face my fellow YPO'ers?" he thought. "What am I going to say to my wife? She was dead set on private school and our child going to college. What am I going to do with the house mortgage?" He couldn't believe he was panicking. "I've got to get a hold of myself," he muttered in an effort to calm himself. "I have been through tough times before, I can get through this as well," he convinced himself.

With solemn resolve he said, "Tomorrow is another day!" and with that he trudged home.

Takeaways:

- Loneliness at the top — *there is a fine line between fear and keeping the employees calm and unafraid.*

- Perception — *How does Bob relay the situation to his leadership team while maintaining authority and imparting confidence?*

- Outsiders —*How will Bob inform his friends, customers and vendors? Will he appear weak? Will vendors have confidence in his abilities to address key issues and resolve them?*

- Getting out of trouble —*Is this situation different than others Bob has faced? Does he need outside help? Should he have reached out earlier?*

- Employees —*What is the best approach for Bob to take to keep his employees from jumping ship and remain productive?*

CHAPTER 6

Crisis Manager

The next morning, Bob called his attorney. After leaving a message, he decided to call the first crisis manager on the bank list.

Gary seemed nice enough and definitely knew how to handle bank special asset departments. He assured Bob that he was on the company's side, but that special assets was a different relationship and needed third party assistance. He decided at that moment, he would meet with him and that he didn't have time to interview others, after all, he thought, time was of the essence.

His attorney, Mark, finally returned the call and agreed to meet the next morning in his office with the crisis manager and Bob (they didn't want the employees to know there was a problem). Fortunately, Mark had a partner who was an insolvency expert and would be at the meeting as well.

The meeting was a blur. Bob couldn't believe this was happening to him. Things were getting out of control.

This was going to be a process all to itself.

Fortunately, the professionals were able to fashion a plan to address the bank, the trade creditors, the customers and, most importantly, the employees.

The discussions about going concern, bankruptcy, fiduciary responsibilities, personal guarantees, employee retainage, business plans, 13-week cash flows, and communication strategies with the bank, creditors and customers had him rattled. So much to do in such a short period of time. He would have to trust others.

The *spinning top* was now in *full wobble*.

Takeaways:

- Business Plans —*Bob recalled from his YPO the need to develop and update his business plans. The strong and fast growth rate of his company blinded him to the necessity of developing and updating his business plans.*

- 13-week cash flow —*The fundamental ideas he learned from his YPO days had never been developed for his own company. While he was aware of the "navigational tools" available to him, his team did not.*

- Bankruptcy – *As the crisis looms, Bob is crushed at the pending thought of bankruptcy. A bankruptcy to Bob equaled ultimate failure.*

- Personal guarantees – *he could lose his house. What does he tell his wife?*

- Communication strategies – *We can't go public with this. What will people think?*

- Crisis manager – *how does he get introduced? Will employees automatically assume the company is in trouble?*

CHAPTER 7

Lessons Learned

Has this ever happened to your business or enterprise? Have things just snuck up and bit you?

The problem with the spinning top is that when it begins to decelerate, it does so at an increasing pace. It begins to wobble.

There are multiple lessons to be gleaned from Bob's story. The key ones are:

1. Complacency
2. Ignoring market trends
3. Ignoring competitive intrusion
4. Absence of ongoing staff training
5. No early warning system
6. Lack of communication among the management team

Bob was successful but perhaps a bit complacent. He had enjoyed a competitive edge in the marketplace, but as he grew from "niche" business to one that had a significant market share, competitors came into his space.

Initially, sales were unaffected, since the market was still growing. But to make room for competition, margins began to slip and customers were able to "double source," so as to have alternative choices.

Sales had to become *value driven* as opposed to order taking. It was important that the company redefine their offering and stay unique in the market place.

Glenn was good at sales. He proved that he could close any deal, once in front of the buyer.

As the company grew, however, his lack of depth in marketing and sales management began to show. He was unable to change his sales offering to adequately compete in the growing competitive landscape.

They lost their competitive edge.

Bill, the general manager, who was a great production manager, was being taxed as a manager. His lack of experience lead to an inability to coordinate sales order entry and backlog into a cohesive operating strategy that integrating sourcing of material, production planning and a shipping strategy.

They began missing shipping dates and had increased stock outs.

Jane, the controller, was essentially an experienced accounting manager. She was taxed getting the accounting work done and the books closed.

The Company had no early warning systems - Dashboards. There were no well thought out business plans and budgets tied to metrics. There was no way to see from week-to-week whether the company was on track. Everything was a surprise when the books finally got closed.

She was NOT a Navigator!

One of the hardest things, as companies grow, is to accurately assess their key people and to either train them to handle the increased size, complexity and speed of the "new" business, or bite the bullet and bring in more talented individuals.

Bob's talents as a CEO, as the company grew, needed to change from a "hands on" manager and solver of all problems to a manager of people.

He needed to develop delegation skills and allow key people to take responsibility AND authority. He needed to develop business metrics and monitor key indicators through a dashboard system, a regularly updated data warehouse where he could see the "early warning" signs.

He needed a real business plan, updated on a regular basis.

The Company needed a new vision and plan of action!

CHAPTER 8

Epilogue

The previous story is an amalgamation of several of the over 120 companies I have helped over the last 20 plus years.

On the first day of an engagement, I often hear, *"Everything was fine until last month when ….,"* or, *"If I only had more capital ….."*

Towards the end of the engagement, hopefully, with a good conclusion, I almost always hear, *"If I only had known what I know today, I would have done everything differently."*

At the end of the day, most CEO's of mid-market companies are dedicated, hard-working people, who have always solved the problem, whatever it has been, on their own. In addition, they have always survived downturns and lived to fight another day.

However, most mid-market CEO's are reluctant to ask for help!

It is lonely at the top. They want to appear positive and leader-like, however they have no one from whom to "bounce ideas." They have no one to really share their concerns and fears. In any businessman's life, both market doubts and self-doubts creep in.

As companies begin to wobble, CEO's often ignore early warning signs (they later regret, but at the moment don't want to appear to be alarmist) and are often afraid to make decisive decisions early in the process and don't give clear instructions (mostly trying to keep "all options" open). This is precisely when they need outside, "objective" help.

Lower middle-market companies, without independent boards and the pressure of being public, often become complacent. The initial vision is not continuously updated and senior management becomes increasingly tactical (day-to-day activities) and less strategic. This can lead to the loss of their competitive edge.

Any plan is better than no plan. As a company grows, so does its complexity and velocity.

The top begins to spin and spin at a more rapid pace. At some point it begins to wobble. If left to fester, it begins to wobble at a greater pace. As the wobble increases it does so at a faster pace.

If a company were a clock, as the dial moves from healthy in the first quadrant, to crossroads in the second quadrant, to conflict in the third quadrant and then into crisis, the number of seconds in each minute decreases.

Wouldn't it be nice if we knew early on when challenges and issues first begin to rise? Wouldn't it be great if we had more time to solve them and come up with the best solutions? Wouldn't it be grand if we could avoid panic?

Read on ......

CHAPTER 9 –

When Life-Cycle and Wobble Collide

Company Life Cycle

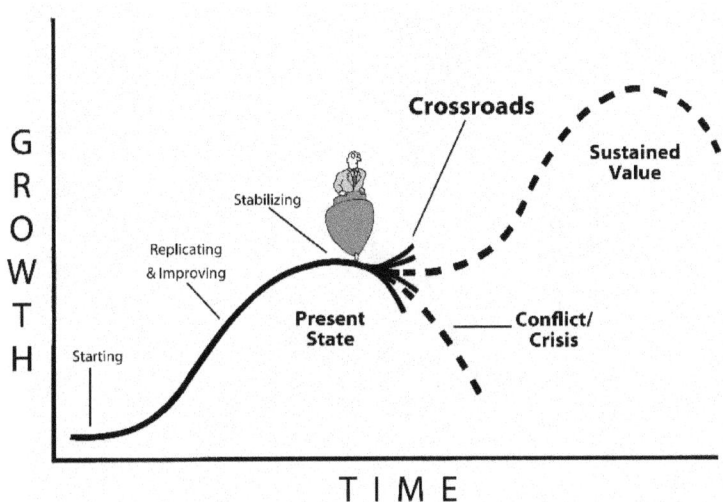

Where are you on the cycle?

Companies need to reinvent themselves in order to foster growth and increase their value. All businesses follow a similar pattern, and reach one plateau after another. If the organization develops the new skills needed, growth continues. Market, economic or technological changes often create a situation where a company is at a crossroads where making the wrong turn can impair future value.

Wobble Cycle:

Wobbles happen when companies go through out-of-the-ordinary events, like sudden growth spurts, loss of key customers or vendors, acquisitions, or other non-ordinary events that tax an owner and his team.

Wobble always starts with a TREMOR, when there are a full sixty seconds in each minute. If undetected and treated, it moves into a QUAKE, where there are now 30 seconds in every minute. Once it becomes a WOBBLE, the company is now running on the edge, things are moving quickly, and if not nimble enough or liquid enough, it will turn into CRISIS.

What happens when these two cycles collide? Read on ….

Chapter 10

Time

Time is a funny commodity. It is easy to waste and impossible to reproduce. Once an opportunity is gone, it is gone.

Imagine a clock, where one to three is "healthy," four to six is "crossroads," seven to nine is "conflict" and 10 to 12 is "crisis." As a company moves around this clock, time speeds up. Or to put it another way, there are less and less seconds in each minute.

This is why when things begin going wrong there is a period when we all go in to panic. Everything seems to be going wrong at the same time. There are too many things to accomplish in a shortened period of time.

Imagine a quarterback, down two touchdowns with six minutes to go. It is a time to slow everything down to make sure every team member is on the same page and begin doing things in a simple, yet decisive manner.

Time is precious. Every company needs to treat it that

way, even in the early part of the clock.

Every company needs a plan that should be clearly understood by all team members, with early warning signals so that there is plenty of time to get the team back on the right track.

Don't wait until there are only six minutes left in the game. Be pro-active. Be a navigator.

Chapter 11

Bad Wobble

It is hard to know exactly where you are on the life cycle curve, but in the case of a serious wobble (or crisis), it can definitely be felt.

Typical symptoms are

- Margins contracting – *increased competition*
- Loss of key customer or vendor – *impact on velocity*
- Liquidity crunch – *vendor pressures*
- Missed business plan – *may need new vision*
- Line of credit maxed – *no wiggle room*
- Personnel increases – *scalability impaired*
- Accelerated growth – *run out of capital*

The company needs to immediately go into a preservation of capital mode. This is where the hiring of a third party professional is paramount, since a lot of decisions, which need to be immediate and decisive, are counter-intuitive to the entrepreneur. Sometimes sacrifices are required to enable a return to growth mode.

Some of the first things to do are to:

- Assess liquidity – *can NEVER run out of cash*
- Develop 13-week cash flow – *navigate liquidity*
- Develop business plan – *define needed capital*
- Buy time to explore options - *negotiate extensions*
- Reduce costs – *develop scalable structure*
- Margins – *identify unprofitable products / customers*
- Leases / Debt – *restructure unnecessary long term debt*
- Meet with senior lender – *enlist their help and support*
- Develop customer strategy – *communicate fixes being made*
- Develop vendor strategy – *enlist help of friendly creditors*
- Sell excess inventory & equipment – *generate cash*

Become a great navigator!

Become even a greater communicator. Don't worry about keeping things quiet so as not to alarm employees, customers or vendors. They already know. Accounts payable clerks are answering vendor calls looking to be paid. Sales and order entry are hearing frustrations from customers on fill rates and late deliveries. The senior lender is monitoring a maxed out borrowing base or full draw on the line of credit.

It is better to acknowledge the elephant in the room with a great plan. Make every key manager part of the solution. Remember, "Idle hands are the devil's playground."

Step up communication with frequency and simplicity!

Chapter 12

Good Wobble - Building Value

Have you ever watched an Olympic downhill skiing racer, or even a professional racecar driver, or even a world champion gymnast? What do they all have in common?

If you answered they are all on the edge of a wobble, you are correct. However, in these cases, it is a controlled and calculated wobble. Let's call this Good Wobble.

The only way to really achieve a world-class organization is to always be challenging yourself and each other. A company has to see itself as a team, practicing every day to achieve world-class performances. Great teamwork and a vision are critical to success.

This is one of the best reasons for bringing in outside, unbiased help. It is imperative that each team member is part of putting together the operating plan and flow. Each employee must know what their role is, how it affects other members of the team and ultimately how it impacts/affects customer satisfaction. There are tremendous synergies that can be achieved by going through this process.

The most empowered organizations understand this. In addition, they build a culture that gives early feedback on both successes and shortfalls, and encourages each team member to push each other. It is important that reasonable goals are set and monitored on a regular basis. No one wants to come to a team meeting not having done his or her part.

Mid-market companies have the biggest challenge moving to this business model. They were typically started from a "garage" and have grown organically. As sales have increased, most mid-market companies react by adding more people to the problem. They assume that everyone is quite busy, but don't realize not every employee is necessarily delivering the most efficient customer experience.

By definition, a well-run and lowest cost organization is only doing those activities that the customer values. Any other efforts are wasted energy.

Getting back to the world-class athletes analogy, they only

train with methods proven to bring them to peak performances. They minimize unnecessary techniques and only focus on those that will deliver a great result.

Likewise, why shouldn't your company do the same?

Companies are either growing or contracting. There is no such thing as standing still.

Steven Jobs said, "Be a yardstick for quality. Some people aren't used to an environment where excellence is expected." *Do your employees emulate this?*

He also said, "Innovation distinguishes a leader from a follower." *Does your company embody this?*

Everything starts with a **great plan and vision**. It is not just simply a budget for the current year and what the senior lender asks for.

A plan is a series of *action items* that define different behavior.

As Einstein said, "The definition of insanity: doing the same thing over and over again and expecting different results."

Does your company fall into this trap?

The moral of the story is – *no businesses are standing still!*

Satchel Paige said, *"Don't look back. Something might be gaining on you."*

There are two critical times when action is needed and when *a company can't afford to be indecisive:*

Preparing for a Liquidity Event – *Maximizing Value*

A liquidity event is any time you are contemplating a re-financing of current debt, bringing in new capital or selling the company. At these times it is important to have:

- Unique sales strategy / branding --- solution selling
- "Lean" organization and strategies
- Systems and reporting to manage / measure growth
- Budgeting that ties to key performance indicators (KPI's)
- Management team capabilities and training

The new investor is looking for innovation and uniqueness, as well as a scalable operation with high potential EBITDA growth.

The second most important time to create or re-visualize value is when things begin to *"Wobble."*

<u>Avoiding *"Wobble"*</u> *– Turning Around Adversity*

- Day-to-day activities consume energies leaving little time for strategic thinking
- New business models or technologies change market dynamics
- Core competencies fail to keep up with need for continuous improvement
- Financial climate changes for completely unrelated reasons

The company must be decisive and time is of the utmost importance. All stakeholders will want to see a well thought out plan and a path back to profitability. They will want to know that there is plenty of time.

Let's get our wobble on!

Chapter 13

Wobble Proofing – It's the People!

Wobbles are usually caused by outside events, but are accelerated and become larger due to inherent defects and quirks that emerge as organizations grow and add new employees with different backgrounds and experiences.

INTERNAL WOBBLES:

An entrepreneurial business can fail, usually not with a bang but with a whimper. As a new business grows, the entrepreneur is involved in every aspect of the business from sales and manufacturing, to order entry and shipping. At some point in this early growth more people are added to perform the different functions as the entrepreneur runs out of bandwidth to do everything.

Over time as more people are added they each bring their own ideas of how a job should be done, and suddenly the care and attention to all the detail is now in the hands of others. The drive of the entrepreneur is dissipated by the number of people that are involved in all of the processes and transactions needed to sell and deliver the product.

The senior people in the organization most likely get on well with the owner, which does not mean that everything they do is effective. Over time these managers introduce their slightly different approach. These changes are not necessarily communicated to everyone, and the information that is needed to make good decisions is often not understood.

Many of the changes made, with the best of intentions, do not make the organization improve. Over time the operating approach will develop a lot of seemingly *minor defects — however, in total they start to make the business more cumbersome and less nimble.*

At this point the owner believes that everything is going well according to his or her view of "how it used to be." As long as the top keeps spinning fast enough it will still appear stable.

In the course of a day, as the entrepreneur realizes that things are not going well, the accumulation of all these minor defects suddenly reveal themselves. The quake that he felt causes the top to start to wobble, and most of the things that they try to do seem to cause the top to wobble even more.

The quake could be one of many things; the loss of a major customer; in a seasonal business the start of the high season; an economic slowdown, etc. For a business that is aware of what is going on around them, none of these events would be fatal. When the focus and attention is dissipated no one sees all of the issues as part of the same situation. Everyone that is in a "control" position is stuck in their-own little silo, and the information needed to avert a problem is spread across a number of functional managers that don't see the whole picture.

Typical outcomes of these problems increase costs, and increase the use of cash; working capital usually increases, again increasing the amount of cash that is tied up; nobody is really listening to customers, and actively receiving the feedback of the bad, and the good, things that are happening; shipments get delayed and the controller is juggling checks. All of the information was in the organization, so why didn't anyone say anything?

Sales knew that the customers were upset about deliveries and product quality; accounting knew that cash was tight; manufacturing knew that they had problems with some poor material.

If there is not enough cash, either expenses had grown too much, margins were lower than they thought, working capital was too high, cash distributions were high, accounts receivable DSO (days outstanding) was too long, factory yields had dropped, etc., etc. None of these things happen overnight!

As you will discover, the most significant breakthroughs will come from within – from the *People Systems*!

A COMPANY'S BEST EARLY WARNING SYSTEM IS PEOPLE AND HOW THEY INTERACT AND SOLVE PROBLEMS ---- THIS IS THE MAGIC OF LOW MIDDLE-MARKET COMPANIES.

EXTERNAL WOBBLES:

The Fix: Build a *PEOPLE BASED* Early Warning System,

through the creation of cross-functional teams at the lower, mid and upper management levels.

Detecting Tremors:

Creating a pro-active, empowered cross-functional team of lower management who are tasked with meeting once a week, at an appointed time (no interruptions). These meetings are predictable and are highly focused. Each member will share un-normal activity at the customer, vendor, operating and financial levels.

This team is typically made up of members from ALL operational and customer facing functions, such as order entry (customer facing), accounts receivable (customer facing), accounts payable (vendor facing), purchasing (vendor facing), operations (plant/process), inventory (product) and shipping/receiving (inbound/outbound activity).

Creating this cross-functional team breaks down the normal silos that occur, allows creative thinking, builds courage and empowers action. More importantly, most problems will resolve themselves at this level, requiring minimum interruption of the CEO and upper management, and minimize events from becoming Wobbles.

Quakes:

Depending on the size and complexity of the company, this could be two teams, one of middle management and another of upper management. In smaller companies, this could be one. At a minimum, this should be a cross-functional team of upper management (CEO direct reports). This is typically made from finance, operations, sales & marketing and human resources. This team also meets weekly at a predetermined time.

Their job is to detect early Quakes and help the Tremor team handle items that become too large for them to handle.

Typically, at least early on, the CEO needs to be informed, however will not have to alter his calendar to dive in. They can come up with solutions, after analyzing the effects on all company operations.

Only after they become larger or out of their charter, does the CEO need to be diverted and directly involved.

At this point, we most likely have handled 90% of all issues before they have significant impact on the organization.

Wobble:

The senior management team, which most likely already meets on a regular basis, will be handling these larger issues. However, as a result of the Tremor and Quake squads (and their efforts), not only does the CEO have an early warning of issues, but can get on top of things before they become a full on Wobble.

The early detection of issues and quick responses keep smaller items and medium size items from becoming large items with limited time to fix. It eliminates the need for organizations to react or fall into crisis.

If you really want to grow your company, your real **systems** and assets are the **people** and the system of **interaction** and problem solving. Your key managers must not only take on additional responsibility, but also be given the same relative increase in authority. The company will need to become an organization of planned risk, as opposed to being risk adverse.

Multiplier Effect:

The magical bi-product from these functioning teams is that they also begin identifying and fixing the defects that cause *Internal Wobble*. The already organized and empowered lower, mid and upper teams begin fixing all those internally created quirks and minor defects by bringing the *PEOPLE SYSTEM* together to solve their own issues.

The company begins to break down the walls and silos between departments. The business begins to get more nimble and far less cumbersome. They will even begin to identify redundancies and unnecessary activities, which will free up capacity and eliminate the need to hire additional people as growth occurs.

Companies need to become organizations of continued improvement, not only in processes but also in empowerment. Mistakes will always happen, but so will progress and great things.

This is the essence of good Wobble.

Chapter 14

Do I Need Outside Help?

CEO's and owners of lower mid-market companies are my heroes. They are personally invested (not a hired hand). Every dollar spent comes out of their pocket, they are proud of their achievements and their success has come from perseverance and hard work.

Before hiring an outsider, other than when in crisis and there is no choice, he needs to ask himself, "Do I have the kind of problem or opportunity that is so bad that ONLY an outside person can help?"

If the answer is yes, the next question should be, "Am I going to get the personal attention of the person I am considering and will my entire organization learn something new from the process (leave behind skills)?"

You should not hire anyone who is a solution in search of a problem. You know your pressure points. You need to be absolutely sure that they are the solution (not the lessor of many evils). You should be confident that they would bring at least 10-15x's their value (enterprise) versus the cost of their services and impact on your organization.

If you can't answer these questions then DON'T hire an outsider.

Make sure that the person who you are talking to will be intimately involved and not just send out a bunch of "experts." Yours is a personal business that needs personal attention.

Rarely are great solutions complicated. Solutions happen because of great buy-in from all team members, a commitment to change for the better and hard work.

All CEOs' and owners have asked, "Why do I always have to generate all new ideas and changes? Why can't I ever get something from my team?" It is lonely at the top, isn't it?

The key is creating an atmosphere where middle management isn't afraid to create change. It starts with empowering them to act as a team and initiate changes. It turns into action when they learn how to work with one another to coordinate the ideas and turn them into action plans.

This is best achieved through outside help. Middle management needs to know that ideas, no matter how crazy they seem, are confidential and that "what happens in the team meetings, stays in the team meetings."

I have found that most breakthroughs come from within. Middle management often has the answers; they just need a stimulus to get them out and into the open. Often times, the most profound solutions start with the most inane thoughts.

It is the job of the consultant to pull these out, help the team map the processes and create action.

So pick the right fit and get started.

Let's have a conversation ....

T

ABOUT THE AUTHOR

Bruce Conklin, Founding Partner of The Fidelis Group, has been involved with the operational and financial restructuring of over 120 companies for more than 20 years. He specializes in full-service financial and operational consulting and has served as Interim Chief Executive Officer and Chief Restructuring Officer for numerous companies in multiple industries.

His clients typically call when *Capital* is constrained (need for new liquidity or loan restructure), *Competitive edge* is lost (brand/sales regeneration), *Operations* need to be transformed into a competitive weapon, *Transaction* is contemplated (maximizing value in sale, acquisition or divestiture), *Conflict* between stakeholders (where value is risked) and *Crisis* needs to be averted.

Prior to founding The Fidelis Group, Bruce was a Principal and Senior Managing Director of Kibel Green Inc., for over 20 years. In addition, he has served as Chief Operating Officer and Chief Financial Officer for several real estate and manufacturing companies. He began his career at KPMG, where he was an Audit Manager, in their New York, Atlanta and Washington DC practices.

Bruce is a Certified Public Accountant and holds a Bachelor of Science from Lehigh University in Bethlehem, Pennsylvania.

Bruce Conklin

www.ingramcontent.com/pod-product-compliance
Lightning Source LLC
Chambersburg PA
CBHW051243170526
45165CB00004B/1549